Kokedama:
A step-by-step guide

Takaaki Kagawa

Copyright © 2015 Takaaki Kagawa

Bonsai Design : Takaaki Kagawa

Cover Design : WriteHit.com

Photos : Alex Bunjes and Takaaki Kagawa

All rights reserved.

ISBN-13: 9781520357461

CONTENTS

0. Preface	1
1. Introduction	3
1.1. Easy bonsai are now in fashion	3
1.2. The prototype of kokedama	3
1.3. Invention of kokedama	5
2. How to make kokedama	7
3. Daily care	13
3.1. Where to keep your kokedama	13
3.2. Watering	13
4. Various types of kokedama	15
5. Other instructions	17
5.1. How to choose mosses	17
5.2. Care and propagation of mosses	18
5.3. How to choose plants	19
5.4. Soil media	21
5.5. Fertilisation	21
5.6. Pests	22
5.7. Repair	22
5.8. Trimming mosses	22
5.9. How long does a kokedama last?	24
5.10. Do we always have to keep kokedama attended?	24
5.11. Hunting plants and mosses	25

0. PREFACE

This ebook is an outcome of my experiment in three countries: Japan, India, and the Netherlands. As a Japanese horticulturist, I had been familiar with some styles of bonsai. There is one particular style which has been popular in Japan, but I only came to know later that some people in other countries are interested in it.

This project started when I tried making a few bonsai in that style in the north of India. At that time, most of the local people I showed them to were not particularly convinced of what I made. They either had their own idea of bonsai or were somehow afraid of them. My bonsai were not the most popular things in North India, but I learnt that it is possible to make them with limited material and even maintain them in an extreme climate with the heat, cold, and rain.

In the meanwhile, I had a chance to make a couple in the Netherlands and Japan as well. I could say these attempts were a success, and I got some positive comments from people. I also found out that there are people outside Japan who are curious to make bonsai in that style, and I decided to write a guidebook for it.

In this ebook, I tried to figure out tips which are applicable in multiple countries, instead of something only people in Japan will find useful. What is fantastic about bonsai is that people can make them with local material, and those can be their own original styles which are not found anywhere else. I hope the readers enjoy this ebook and also enjoy making these bonsai.

Takaaki Kagawa
Author

1. INTRODUCTION

1.1. Easy bonsai are now in fashion

A bonsai is a miniature landscape with a planting, which is believed to have originated during the Tang dynasty of China or even earlier. Many people who know a bit about bonsai think they include little trees which take a lot of time and effort to maintain. It is true in some cases, but not entirely so. There are other kinds of bonsai which are easier to maintain and quicker to make as well. Bonsai are moving on as people's lifestyles change.

In Japan, a style of casual bonsai called *kokedama* (pronounced *co-keh-dah-mah*) have been popular these days. These bonsai stand without pots and have herbs, grasses, or small shrubs, including common house plants. In the past, only people who had plenty of time and money like rich old people owned bonsai. But it has become a popular fashion in the country since a simple of modern and lower-maintenance styles were invented.

1.2. The prototype of kokedama

The prototype of kokedama is believed to be a form of bonsai called *ne-arai* (pronounced *neh-ah-rye*), which can be translated into 'root washer' or 'washed roots'. During the political period called *the Edo Period* (1603-1867), someone came up with an innovative idea of creating a potless bonsai. There is nothing to contain the soil, and the soil and the plant roots are exposed. You might wonder how that can even work, but the trick is that the well-developed roots of the plants hold the soil together. The surface of the soil is sometimes covered with moss. The lack of pots gives the unbelievable presentation as well as the advantage that you don't need expensive pots, because some pots for bonsai can cost a fortune and be much more expensive than the plants.

There are a few different methods to make ne-arai. One way of making them is to pull out a potted plant with circulated roots from the pot, re-shape the bottom part if needed, and mature them with the roots exposed. Another way is to make them without a pot from the beginning and let the plants grow roots. The second method takes less time and gives more options for shapes and sizes, but it needs more care until the plants develop enough roots to hold the soil together.

This style of bonsai must have surprised people when they first appeared. They became popular in Japan and are still made and appreciated today. There are various kinds of ne-arai, and it is very common these days to make them with herbs, grasses, or small shrubs, because they tend to grow much faster than trees, and also the Japanese have the culture of appreciating wildflowers.

A ne-arai with grasses

1.3. Invention of kokedama

Kokedama (pronounced *co-keh-dah-mah*) can be translated into 'moss ball', and these are often classified as easier and quicker versions of ne-arai. A kokedama is basically a planted ball of soil covered with live moss, and this style of bonsai have gained popularity since the early 2000s. But it is not clearly known who originally came up with the idea, and there are a couple of individuals who claim to be the first one to have created them. According to some sources, Isao Umiji, a horticulturist, invented kokedama in the late 1990s.

Today, kokedama are so popular in Japan that they are even appreciated among those who had never been expected to show interest in bonsai. Every year, many kokedama classes are held in Japan. They look nice just as they are, but you can also display them on a nice glass/ceramic plate or with other accessories.

Grass kokedama in different sizes

2. HOW TO MAKE KOKEDAMA

Before assembling a kokedama, there are a couple of things to do. First, choose the soil media. You can use various types of media according to what kinds of plants you are using. Choices would be garden soil, dry sphagnum, peat, or a mixture of multiple media, but they have to be something that stays together when you make a ball. Make sure that your soil media are pest-free. Earthworms are a pest in kokedama because they make tunnels inside the structure and damage it.

Next, prepare the moss. Wash it carefully and clean it. When you are using a long, fluffy moss, it will make the work easier later if you break up the clumps, make a 'moss sheet', and dry it for a day, which you can make wet later when you use it. But if you are using a very short moss, it is probably better to keep the clumps as they are.

A moss sheet drying on a mesh

The plants you are planning to use should also be washed and cleaned (mosses are also plants, but here we distinguish them for clarity). Wash off the old soil and remove the old roots. Cut off some of the roots if they are too long.

The method to make a kokedama is to cover the roots of plants with soil media, make it into a tight ball, cover it with live moss, and then tie the ball with a dark-coloured organic thread very thoroughly. Make sure that the ball of the soil mixture is not loose, otherwise it may soak up water and 'melt' later, particularly if you are using muddy media. The ends of the thread can be tucked into the ball. After that, give it a generous shower until the water coming out is clear.

Step 1: Wash and clean the plant(s)

Step 2: Make a tight ball around the roots of the plant(s)

Step 3: Wrap the ball with moss

Step 4: Tie the ball and the moss together with organic thread

Step 5: Give it a shower until the water comes out clear

As the moss grows, the thread around the kokedama will be covered up, and the thread itself will also be gone. The moss at the bottom of a kokedama will usually die. If you find that wasteful, you can use some other materials like a mesh to hold the soil at the bottom.

Moss covering the surface of a kokedama

There are a couple of common mistakes that people make. One of such mistakes is using too many plants in one kokedama. It is crucially important to be modest about it because the plants will grow bigger and become overcrowded after a while. Another mistake is to use too much moss. It will initially look greener and more beautiful if you use a lot of moss, but it will start coming off after a while because only the new growth can hold on to the soil surface. The old bits of the moss in contact with the soil media will end up dead without doing much. It is not a problem if some of the soil surface is visible on a new kokedama.

The bigger a kokedama is, the easier it is to take care of unless it is ridiculously huge. Smaller ones need a lot more attention than larger ones, but they are easier to make or transport and occupy less space. You will probably have to plan the size somewhere in between. You should also consider the ultimate sizes of the plants you are using, although this can be controlled to some extent by the amount of fertiliser.

A snowrose kokedama

3. DAILY CARE

3.1. Where to keep your kokedama

You can keep them in a place which is suitable for the plants/moss. Don't shut them in an airtight room as they need some fresh air. If your region has very hot seasons, you might have to protect them from burning sunlight. In cold winter, it would be better to move them indoors to protect them from freezing.

3.2. Watering

You can water kokedama just like ordinary potted plants by giving them showers every day. Make sure that all the moss evenly gets water, otherwise there will be parts of the moss which don't grow well.

Many people also soak the spheric part of them in water every couple of/few days just to make sure that the plants get enough water. This is optional, but it is effective in the hot/dry season when water evaporates quickly. Be careful, however, not to leave them in water for a long time. Some kokedama can melt or dissolve when you leave them in water and forget about them, and the plants and mosses that we use for these things probably don't like being drenched in water for too long.

4. VARIOUS TYPES OF KOKEDAMA

These days, some Japanese people make special types of kokedama with aquatic plants and mosses. You can grow them in an aquarium, an aqua-terrarium, or even a garden pond. Hanging kokedama are also interesting. You can tie a kokedama with hemp thread and hang it, or you can embed a hook in a kokedama when you make it and then hang it. Another type of kokedama are the ones without plants. There is no such rule that a kokedama must have a plant. However, these ones could be slightly fragile. You can mix something fibrous in the soil to make the structure strong.

A kokedama with Ficus pumila

5. OTHER INSTRUCTIONS

5.1. How to choose mosses

There are a countless number of moss species in the world. Among which, the best types of mosses for kokedama would be creeping mosses which have thready stem-like structures attached with tiny leaves. These creeping mosses are the easiest ones to deal with as they cover the soil surface and hold it. Some of erect mosses are also good as long as they are not too long/tall. They will grow in clumps and slowly cover the soil surface. Liverworts and hornworts may not be suitable. Mosses found in very wet environments should probably be avoided as well, because they tend to need a lot of water or an extremely humid condition.

Mosses are mostly found in gardens, forests, or sometimes even in streets. If you are lucky, you can even buy them. It is best if you can find fresh green moss, but otherwise dry moss is good enough as long as it still has some sign of life. If the moss is completely brown, there are chances that they are dead.

You can mix different types of mosses. However, there is a possibility that just one or two varieties will be dominant and the others will lose their niche. If you are worried about that, it is best to use just one type of it.

Moss

5.2. Care and propagation of mosses

Mosses often prefer misty/humid conditions because they need to absorb water from their bodies. They don't have roots to pump up water like flowering plants do. Some mosses are OK with some sunlight, and many others prefer shades. When you collect moss by yourself, note what kind of environment you find it in.

They also need fresh air, instead of being locked up in an airtight room. When the air is dry, misting or frequent watering will keep them healthy. However, most of them can survive without water for a while. You can even dry leftover moss, keep it in a cool and dark place, and soak it in water when you need it next time.

Mosses multiply with microscopic spores, instead of seeds. However, you can easily propagate them from pieces of their bodies. When you can't find an adequate amount of the variety of moss you need, you can propagate it by chopping it up or pulling it apart, sprinkling it on soil without adding fertiliser, and keeping it in an appropriate place while frequently giving it a mist or a gentle shower. Most mosses tend to grow slowly, so be patient if it takes a while before you have enough of it for kokedama.

When you use wild moss collected from a garden or natural site, wash and clean it in water and, if possible, dry it for a day or two in a shade to avoid any infestation. It would also be better to use the kinds of mosses that grow in the same conditions as the plants you are planning to grow in your kokedama.

When your moss is not looking good, it can just be seasonal. Mosses often slow down or change colours in the dry and cold seasons. Otherwise, the moss may be kept in a wrong environment or infected. Cut off the damaged parts and wait for it to grow back. Try to keep the kokedama in an environment which is closer to that of the place where you found the moss. You could look it up if you have a clue which kind of moss it is.

A horsetail kokedama

5.3. How to choose plants

Basically, you can use any plants as long as they can grow in a kokedama without big problems. One of the most important things is to use plants that can grow in the media of your choice and can coexist with the moss. That means you need to use plants that can grow in the same environment as your moss, and the media should be appropriate for both of them. Another important point is to use plants which are easier to maintain. If you choose a wrong plant, you may have to spend time with unnecessary things.

The most suitable plants for kokedama would be those with many fine roots, such as grasses, sedges, ferns, and many others. Those will hold the soil media better. The size of the plants is also important. Choose the ones which are less likely to outgrow the kokedama you are planning to make. Otherwise your kokedama might end up in a huge pot or in your garden soon.

You should pay attention to the life cycle of the plants as well. If you want to enjoy the same plants all year round, use something evergreen. Otherwise, you could plant something seasonal and enjoy the change. It is also nice if you can use both the types of plants in the same kokedama.

Bulbous/tuberous plants can do well in kokedama, but you should be careful because some of them might deform the kokedama after a season, when they start forming new bulbs or rhizomes inside the structure. Fast-growing climbers or creepers may not be suitable because they have the potential to end up everywhere and keep you busy with scissors. If you are using succulents, they should be chosen carefully because some of them don't do well in kokedama. But some types of Sedum would be an option for example. Some small kitchen/medicinal herbs make good kokedama. Many of them have a fragrance, and they are not only practical but also nice to look at.

Some plants easily die from having their roots disturbed. When you use such plants, sow a seed on the top of a 'plain' kokedama with no plants. In this way, you can introduce these kinds of delicate plants in kokedama without damaging the roots.

A violet flowering on a kokedama

5.4. Soil media

Any soil medium or mixture is good as long as the plants/moss don't react against it. Some media are more acidic while others are more alkaline, and some media hold more water while others tend to drain it. You should check if your medium and plants/moss match each other before you make a kokedama. When you use garden soil, sterilise it with heat, and then cool it down before using it. You can also dry it completely under direct sunlight.

5.5. Fertilisation

You can use liquid fertiliser dissolved in water when you water your bonsai. However, you should keep the concentration low because strong fertiliser can damage the moss and over-fertilise the plants as well. For the ratio, the concentration for orchids would be good enough in most cases.

5.6. Pests

Anything that can damage the plants or the soil structure can be a pest. Earthworms make tunnels in the soil structure, and birds can pull out the moss from your bonsai. Some insects, other bugs, or fungi can damage the live materials. Try to keep them away from your bonsai or use pesticide, according to the type of the pest.

5.7. Repair

When you need to repair or size up a kokedama, remove the moss on the surface, add more soil, cover it with live moss, and tie it thoroughly in the same way you make new kokedama. You can use the moss you have removed from the old surface unless it has a problem.

If the moss gets peeled off the soil surface, you can just tie it back with dark-coloured organic thread. If necessary, remove the dead old layer of the moss underneath the live part with a pair of scissors.

5.8. Trimming moss

When the moss has grown out of shape or uneven, you need to trim it. You should also do it when the moss becomes too thick, otherwise the unexposed part of the moss under the surface will die, and the layer of moss can come off like a peel one day. Just trim it evenly with a pair of scissors. You don't have to do this very often as moss is not something that rapidly grows overnight.

Before trimming:

After trimming:

5.9. How long does a kokedama last?

It is not easy to decide how long you can enjoy a kokedama. The answer is, it is up to you. Even if the plants die, you can plant a new one or even sow a seed.

5.10. Do we always have to keep kokedama attended?

Ideally, we should take care of kokedama every day, but there must be times you have to leave them for a few days. If nobody is available to take care of them during your absence, you can, for example, keep your kokedama on an old wet towel with one end stuck in a bucket of water so that water can be supplied. Make sure that you don't leave them where the water is going to dry up soon or lock them up in a room which is completely shut.

You can also solve this problem to some extent by choosing plants which can survive in dry environments. A fern-like plant called *Selaginella tamariscina*, for example, has the ability to dry up completely and then resume growing whenever it gets water. In addition, many mosses are tolerant of temporary water shortage. When you water dried moss, it will absorb the water and start growing again.

5.11. Hunting plants and moss

Using wild plants/moss isn't necessary. But when you hunt plants/moss, it would be better to do it near the place you live in or even in your own garden, rather than in a remote place with no trace of human life. This is because the plants/moss from your neighbourhood would adjust better to your environment than those from a place which is very different from yours. You should also avoid causing too much damage to the local ecosystem. For example, it would be better to collect a few seeds and grow them than to uproot mature plants.

Don't hunt plants/moss in an owned/protected land without permission. Otherwise you might face legal trouble. You should also avoid collecting endangered species from habitats. Check the status of the land or the plants in advance when you plan a trip to the place.

A camellia kokedama

ABOUT THE AUTHOR

Takaaki Kagawa has been providing advice to authors of botanical/horticultural books and articles published in Japan. Takaaki has been a plant enthusiast since the age of seven, when he found a book on carnivorous plants at the school library. He is also the author of *Living with Plants*, a horticulture/gardening e-guidebook and *Drosera of Japan*, a botanical reference on Japanese sundews.

Printed in Poland
by Amazon Fulfillment
Poland Sp. z o.o., Wrocław